Awakening

the

Other Side

poems and art illustrations

Michelle Hanna

In Time Publications, Inc.

Published by In Time Publications Inc.
          P.O. Box 190537
          Ft. Lauderdale, FL 33319

Printed in the United States of America

Scripture taken from the New King James Version. Copyright ©
1979, 1980, 1982 by Thomas Nelson, Inc. Used by permission. All
rights reserved.

Quoted line on page 2 taken from song titled "I Want You" by Marvin
Gaye.
Quoted line on page 18 taken from song titled "Ain't No Sunshine" by
Bill Withers.

Cover and About The Author photos by Don Parchment
Cover design by La Toya A. Atkins
Interior design by Lee Lewis, Words Plus Design
Art Illustrations by Erle Bethell and Michelle Hanna

Library of Congress Cataloging Card Number: 2004098155
ISBN: 0-9762857-0-3

Dedicated
To
You

~

To Darlene,

Best Wishes

M.Hanna
2008

"Not what goes into the mouth defiles a man; but what comes out of the mouth, this defiles a man."

— Matthew 15:11

Contents

Foreword

There comes a time when something new…something fresh…something daring…must have an opportunity to breathe. And if denied that chance…we are all the less for it. When poets walk this land they walk calmly…courageously…with compassion and wisdom.

We are all so fortunate that poets come when we need them…not necessarily when we want them. Michelle is such a voice…clear…concise…brave…uncompromising…here to ring the bell of truth to say that our people have a right to the tree of life.

It is a pleasure to see any sunrise…any sunset…. They come every day even when it is cloudy and we do not see them. It is a pleasure to be here at the dark dawning of a wonderful, loving poet. Good for all of us who love poetry…but more…good for all of us who love life.

— Nikki Giovanni
October 2004

Prologue

I create my world with words
Words written, words spoken
Words from my heart
Manifesting when they depart
Words never disappear
Silent they seem but loud they are heard
They enter into a dimension
Waiting for execution
Then into the atmosphere
Traveling in the pockets of air
Like seeds they settle in the soil of the earth
Out of its shell it is released
Piercing the ground with its feet
Causing the fruit it contains to be produced
The product of every word I speak

Souls Introduced

The story has already been written, in a time of old
Even before our souls were introduced
Our spirits have been guided to what has been told
So many phenomenon, even before,
Still after, strange but true
But I don't believe in coincidence
I believe what is, is supposed to be
A higher power controls the universe,
Has already worked out the things,
Which will be, even before it is seen

Seems like our minds intertwine, it's like
I see into yours and you see into mine
We walk the same line, yet I trail behind
I feel the energy pulling me to you
I follow where it leads, yet I don't know what it means
I see the unseen, but I don't know what the end will be
I wonder: do you feel the same, do you have a clue
I call things only God gives command to,
Somehow it involves you

Only God knows where the winds go
I ask God and he shows me truth
But I'll follow through till the end
I don't know what you prayed for,
But mine came true
Spiritually we are truly connected
Do you see the things I see?
I don't know if you know,
But these things, can't only be happening to me
Can you feel me?

awakening the other side

A Spiritual Connection

When two people meet the energy that is felt,
It's chemistry, a feeling like there's just something about
    you,
Something that makes you stare, makes you wanna be
    near,
Like I've known you before
This crave, makes me want more

Something physical happens though
A kind of body language that lets the person know,
I'm checking you out
You make yourself available to observe and be seen
The eyes can magnetize
Watching them makes you laugh inside
The passion burns and Marvin plays in my head
    "I Want You"

A spiritual connection, the energy between two,
Can be felt from a distance
So much can be said without words spoken
But without words to confirm
Those emotions leave you hesitant,
What is hidden behind the stares?
Action needs to be taken

You question, where is this going to lead?
Will the connection be lost because words weren't
    exchanged?
This is not the intention
So much needs to be said
Things that can only be expressed,
Through two people being in the same place,
Making us able to communicate

In my mind a voice cries
We should meet and discuss the desires that be
Sparks will fly from the fire that burns in me
No need to worry it will be heavenly
All hidden is true
Wow, you and me, that's like a dream
Under the sun or moonlight,
It really doesn't matter; I just want you close to me

3

awakening the other side

awakening the other side

Hidden

More than skin deep
It's your spirit I seek
More than what meets the eyes
It's about the soul of you

More than physical attraction
It's about what the mind speaks
More than feelings
It's about expressing

It's not about what a person represents
It's about the mere essence of you
More than what words can say
It's about the action one takes

More than the whispers
It's about the message taken
Not about where you are
It's about who surrounds you

Not about what the mind sometimes assumes
Live beyond that
It's about finding and understanding truth

Rise above, the negative people say
It's about harmony, the unification of one love for you
    and me
Not about what money can buy
It's about what money cannot
It's about love is love

Not about the present, it's about destiny
Not about what's seen, but what's unseen
Not about short term, but everlasting

awakening the other side

awakening the other side

Distant Love

My love rendition
It's a spirit-to-spirit transmission
No matter the distance
My love can reach
Because I speak to your heart without speech
Even though I can't touch
I still feel so much
Through mystical sensory
My spirit travels over seas and mountains
To my heart's desire burning on fire
Love has no end or boundary
So the energy transcends higher and higher

I'm like a cloud
I'll shower you with love
When the showers fall
All the butterflies come alive inside
I shiver, making it known love has arrived
Everlasting, unconditional
Like a mother loves a child
That makes heaven smile
Love gives all that it can give
Which is one hundred percent
The substance of why we live
Time tells, love always reveals
All of its intents

Strangers yet a familiar presence of you
Fills my soul
How could this be? I wonder
It is beyond my control
Only heaven can send
Straight from above

A kind of love of such rarity
Innocent and precious like a dove
To show love in its full capacity
God's will orchestrates to demonstrate
The power of love
Or maybe I knew you in heaven
A long time ago

Providence

You are my coincidence
Those events that flash from my subconscious
Blinking seconds too ambiguous to hold
But then the reoccurrence of imagery extends,
Steering my actions, giving directions to where I need to
     stand
In accordance to God's purpose and plans
But before one of those events came alive
I had to have those events visualized

So can I dream you here?
Compel the energy to bring you near
When I open my eyes inside
Tuning you in to my reception
Do our signals coincide?
When my body quivers is it you I feel
Charging through me flowing like a river
This field of force I can't repel

Am I your coincidence?
Those little moment-to-moment incidences
That penetrates your intellect with questions
To look deeper into what is happening
Which brings you closer to the One who organizes
To get a glance from God's eyes

awakening the other side

Obscure

More concern about what it looks like on your behalf
It makes me behave in a way I'm not sure you can
    recognize
It is obscure and these glimpses can't paint the true
    picture
But every moment my eyes hold and capture
I paste the episodes bit by bit, piece by piece
Waiting for it to be complete

But with you it seems like I don't exist
Because my chances always come up amiss
Maybe something is underlying that you continue to
    conceal
Or maybe what I see and believe is lying to me

These pages taste my tears as they turn and turn
My stories mean one thing to me and something else to
    others
So I guess it is purposed beyond this
It evolves creating a new meaning I'm still learning
It keeps me driven to reveal what is hidden

The gap is wide and it doesn't seem to be closing in
Maybe another level of circumstance
Will remedy this situation
Because with my mind I can't understand what this means
It tells me to let go
And maybe it won't make a difference
If I leave or stay
Because your life will go on like it should
But you'll never know what could have been

But then my heart holds on with all its might
Because I want you so bad
And that leads me to playing it safe
Like chess I contemplate
About all the right moves to make
So I'm going to loosen my grip
Let caution flip
Take risk with guided wisdom
Be not afraid of losing what is yet to come
Because fear won't be the reason
I don't walk towards and complete the undone
Only the appointed time and season
God's will, my will and your will then it will be done
So let it be

awakening the other side

Undying

Where can I find you, love?
For I've walked among your people
And in your town, yet could not be found
Until love surrenders, from a distance I linger
Not to wait in vain, I pray
I hope fate delivers you my way
But until time is in line and calculations
Of all that needs to be
I'll step into what is truly mine
Whenever you need love, you'll find me

For many moons have shone
And its kisses have been blown
I view your eyes in a dying sun,
That is continually reborn
With the passing of time, love will still show
Like the sun faithful in its burning glow

Even if I don't possess your love
It doesn't stop the love that flows
It will never cease, love goes on until eternity
And it doesn't depend on you loving me
It is strong, yet it yearns, to love and be loved in return

Kiss of The Moon

The sun slowly crosses the horizon
As it fades another light arises
A gentle flow of breeze on the trees
Fill the air with the scent of jasmine
The moon in its bloom blows a kiss to you
Beautifully whispering to your heart
May I come in?

A new day lies ahead
Full of promises to fulfill
Listen to your heart, obey what it says
All that you feel inside do not hide
Be wise let truth be your guide
Follow through steadfast, binding
Speak what's in your heart, that's what you'll find
Something beautiful is at the end
When you possess what you've discovered
Hold tight, don't let it blow in the wind

Memories of you linger in my mind
Fresh like morning dew
Like the tide caressing the shore,
I need to touch you
Memories can create fantasies
I want what is real
My lips await sugar from yours
Heavily poured
I long for you more and more

awakening the other side

The quest starts and ends with you
Time waits for no one
Yet patience is a virtue
A time and season for everything
And like preservation of vintage wine
The best result is of time
Still I wait for you

awakening the other side

Silent Serenade

Gazing through eyes to galaxies
Beyond the beyond
Like a frozen pond I glide and dance on
Bypassing the rigid cold of my solitude
To the warmth of summer's high noon

Stretching thoughts to tickle your heart
Hoping you'll hear my silent serenade
Attention to laughter, please bring
Remembrance of me even after
The smile fades

Oh burdensome clouds tell me how long
Have you swallowed your cry to
Have an outburst of silver tears to fall
Heavily like mine

I summon a whirlwind to carry my sigh
Sit it down at your sides
Bring it up from the ground swirling
Let you inhale my exhale
So you'll know what it feels like
When you're not around

Sunshine

As the rain dances on rooftops
And the smell of the earth cleansing
I think about bathing in your love
Heaven pours out blessings
To nurture the ground
Spring forth life that is abound
Into my life a flower I've found
You are the light that shines with laughter
Just like when it rains the promise
Of the rainbow comes after
I promise you
That is why I sing this song
"Ain't no sunshine when she's gone"

Je T'aime Mon Amour

On a tree lap a man sits
With his guitar in hand, he begins to play it
His fingers caressed the strings
As if it was his lover's hair
To his lady he sings

Je t'aime, Je t'aime, je t'aime
Mon amour
Je t'aime, Je t'aime, je t'aime
Mon amour

The melodies amidst the trees resonated
Through the leaves vibrating their limbs
Into a ballet dance

Je t'aime, Je t'aime, je t'aime
Mon amour
Je t'aime, Je t'aime, je t'aime
Mon amour

His passionate stare
Gave a voice to her heart with a language
Only spoken through her eyes
Saying…

Across a desert sky cuddled by a melody
We'll enter through a portal
From mortal to immortal
With a wink of an eye
There we'll make our beds to lie
We'll fluff the clouds like pillows
Have eternal dreams without slumber
With no remembrance of yesterday or tomorrow

Divine Love

You have taken residence,
Consumed my mind
No matter what I do
I can't shake you
Thoughts of you bleed from my brain
Enter into my veins
Now you're breathing, living in my soul
Strangely, I feel you so close
But you I can't hold

What is your fear?
How could something so pure and true,
Scare you?
Fear is a thief, stealing all that is precious
Have you thinking of pain when there is none
Tries to take everything away when it just begun
Don't let it come between and divide
Fear was not given to us
So don't let it control what you feel inside

Heaven's appointed time led me to you
An intentional whisper
Have two spirits merging into one
My dreams came true when I came to know you
A familiar feeling takes me
Back to when I was young
When I made a cry to heaven
For someone like you

What we have is a rare occurrence,
Something that was foretold
Precious like stones from beneath the earth,
Priceless in worth
Full of splendor so sublime
You can spend your lifetime to find
To cherish and hold
Because things like this, doesn't happen all the time

awakening the other side

Love Triangle

When things don't work out
Between you and she
You come crawling back to me
With all the mess
Love shouldn't be with conditions
Or decisions of who shall it be
Real love is unconditional
It's what I've given you,
And want back for me

Why should I put up with this mess?
I know I deserve the best
Caught in between
Waiting to see, whom will you choose?
Is it she or me
Who has the best of this sick relationship?
Maybe it's you, tormented between two

I had enough of this love triangle episode
I don't need this
Because the love inside of me is higher
I'm strong and I'll survive this
I can walk away without regrets
Or reasons why
'Cause all the evidence is clear
That you don't belong to she or me
Now all of your selfishness leads you to
No comfort from neither one, she nor me

Over You

I'm over you
For the first time I can see the sun
Love comes and goes
But for now I'm done

No romance, I just wanna be free
I'm over you
No more heartaches and pain
This love has been a battlefield
A losing game

I hang my flag in the wind
Indications I've given in
Not to let heartache win

Now I set my standards high
Not to fall for the games people
Play these days
Fear in the hearts of many is the cause
Of the many hearts they choose
To abuse and bruise
Like a prey caught in their claws
They manipulate and devour innocent faces
Only to fulfill their empty spaces

Let Love

Let love flow, let it reach where it ought to go
Give no thought, to whom you should love,
Spread love to all you know
Let love burn in your soul
Keep it on your brain like a stain
It is universal and it is free
Let's accept and give it back, please

Love is all we need,
To understand the mysteries
Perfect love has no fear
Whisper, I love you, in the ear
Of the person next to you
Light the fire, let's create a flame
Let it melt away the callous,
Rid all heartless
Turn tears to gladness
If tears shall fall let them be from joy

Let love rule in you
Give in to love, let it cultivate
Be radical, love the one you hate,
It will emancipate
Frowns will turn to smiles after awhile
You'll see the difference that it can make
Rid all sorrows,
Because no one is promised tomorrow
Let love come alive, let us live like it's our last

Sharing, caring, being of one unity
Giving thanks and praise to God who created all
This world can be a better place for you and me
A paradise for all the eyes to see

awakening the other side

awakening the other side

It's A Crime

We both know, it wouldn't last
'Cause I'm with him and you're with her
Romancing on the down low,
Moment to moment hurts us both
It's a crime to love someone who belongs to another
Still we let our desires lead to deceive
Saying one more night then we'll let go
But one last kiss, leads to one more night of bliss
We both know we're wrong,
'Cause we both have families at home

Private meetings, hoping no one will see
Living without regrets, as it seems
We let our desires get the best of us
Delighting in pleasure, betraying our trust
Realizing this passion must end
Ignoring the obvious
We got careless and let our covers be seen
Now we must face the consequences
And bear all that we feel against losing our marriages

Now we're dancing to a sad song
Every note haunts us to the bone
Saying we should have, could have, if only we would
      have let it go
Now we're both on our knees begging our loved ones
Please baby please, don't leave

awakening the other side

Midnight Tears

Midnight pain causes my eyes to cry
No one is there only an invisible but touchable God
Who takes away all that I cannot bear
The morning listens to my sigh
When I stretch my arms to snuggle the sky
Engulfed by the abyss
I bless it with a kiss

Sometimes I question what is going on
Without the utterance of why
Because I know certain things have to take place
Before the manifestation
But sometimes my eagerness lessens my patience
So I get lost in frustration
I just want your arms to console me
Talk with you till the dawn comes
Watch the awakening sun

But I won't settle for less
I must get what I want
Even if the process prolongs
I'll keep holding on
But all in God's time
So let God's will be done
And I'll continue to cry until you're mine

Morning Song

When morning yawns
Peep her dawn
The only sound in the air,
Are the birds' songs
When the sun fully show its face
Fragments of silence disappear
Echoes of car horns fill your ear

In the kitchen smells
Of eggs and coffee brew
In the living room
Highlights of the news
On the streets, kids
Talking, walking to school

As morning stretches her arms
I lie in bed
Wondering what shall I wear
I rather stay in bed and at the
Ceiling stare
But productive I need to be
So out of bed I roll me

Into the bathroom I dash
Like the morning air, I refresh
Pray to God for this day to be blessed

awakening the other side

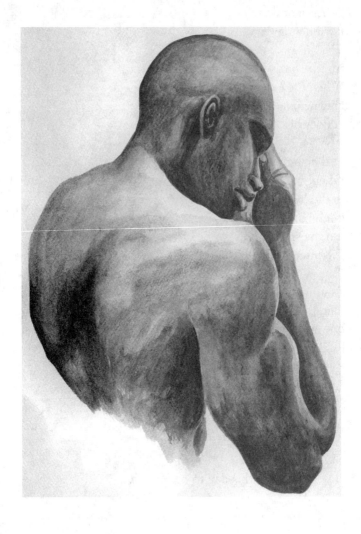

My Disgrace

My hands to my face, I'm full of disgrace
All the hurt I've caused
Now my wife wants a divorce
It is too much for her to bear
The cheat falls on all
Taken away all the happy times
We would have shared

What will our kids say
About us going our separate ways?
I acted so selfishly
Now I'm about to lose my family

They're too young to understand
What kind of characteristics I display as a man
Our kids will be torn between two
This is not the life I promised you

I knew this would happen
But I let lust take control
Now my heart is scarred
So I have to turn to God
For He is the only one
That can bring back what I've lost

Love Like Before

We don't talk, laugh much anymore
We used to be inseparable
It used to be struggles, but with joy
Where have all the good times gone?
Through the years we let the fire die
Taking each other for granted is what we do best
    nowadays
The old days I miss when we appreciated our first kiss

The comfort of love resides
But the passion isn't alive
Our eyes only see what please us,
We think it's better on the other side
But heartaches and pain lie just the same
When lust overtakes destruction is gained

Now the silence is screaming in my ear
Telling me something needs to be done
Let's rekindle the flames, make it,
Like our younger years
When there were hardly any heartaches and tears

I remember walking hand and hand,
Everywhere we went, long talks till morning came
Dinner for two with a single rose for you

We can still have it like before because love never dies
It's only our fire burning dim
With effort we can remove the pain
'Cause I remember when love was fun
Hidden messages around the room
Candle lit dinner in fancy lingerie awaits you after a long
    day

Let's take it back to when the fire burned more
When I couldn't wait to be at your door
Dozen roses just to brighten your day
Gifts not only on holidays
Sweet words whispered in your ear
Saying, I love you dear

awakening the other side

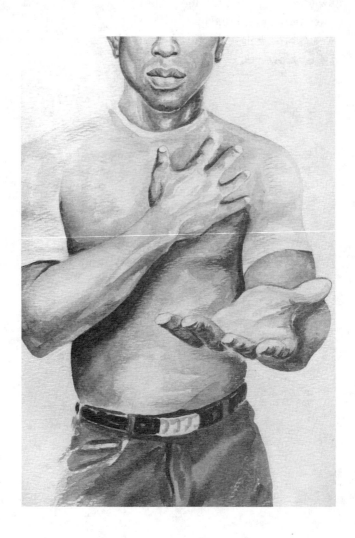

Come My Love

Life is too short for hesitations
Let us not waste time
Let us connect again
I know you feel the same
Because you're reading my mind
I can only do what you allow
Besides that, I need you now

I'll meet you anywhere at anytime
Just say the words and I'll be there
We've got so much to share
Come feel, taste this love
Being sung through poetry
Let our chemicals mingle like chemistry
Let us see what you and I are made of
When we unite, it'll be like dynamite
Fireworks will explode, a release of pure delight

To heaven and back
An excess of love will never be lacked
If I'm what you need
Then you should call me
Come feel this fire
I know you're burning for me
Like I'm for you
Because I can feel the heat
So come, let's make this destiny complete

I ache for the soothing softness of you
You in my eyes make them come alive
I'll be all you want me to be
Whatever you go through I'll go through
Whatever you feel I'll feel too

A kind of love like whatever happens to you
Feels like it happens to me too
When that time comes, when it is you I see
My inside will shout
This is what love is about
But one thing I'm asking, just hold me tight
Because I'll feel like I'm about to pass out

Romantically

I love you...
Those three words I don't use carelessly
Because they mean so much to me
I save them for precious moments
Like in the act of lovemaking
When your heart is overflowing
Then love starts to drip from your eyes
And you hold on for your dear life
Bodies sink into one another
'Cause you don't ever want to let go

Wrapped up in the afterglow
Burning, yearning, crying joy
Cause it feels that good
At this time those words could never be misunderstood
Your heart starts yelling...I want you, I need you
A protective feeling overwhelms
Like I could never hurt you
For you, I'll go to any measure
To bring in every way you pleasure
Because that is where I find my treasure

So much time in between
Will you stick around or
Get bored and carry on?
Over 365 days have gone
Yet still I wait with anticipation
For our face to face conversation
My vision has not gone hazy
Because I'm still missing, wanting,
Needing you like crazy

awakening the other side

A Love Story

Created before time begun
Before my eyes have seen
Before the music has played
You were embedded in my soul
The alignment of heaven
With its gravitational force,
Is now manifesting what I can hold

A story written destined for things
My imagination can't comprehend
Forbidden are the things my mind can't erase,
The fantasies I create, which can't compare
To what is in store for this love affair

The scenes setup with precision
With the right amount of light leading
The characters in as they are introduced
Playing their parts reading from a script,
A Great Hand produced

I accept this love with open arms
Waiting with patience to encounter all of its charms
Unraveling the mysteries of what must be
The disappointments to advancements
Through the challenges make you
Feel you deserve... the rewards of persistence

If our paths didn't meet
I would have never kissed your cheek
And my pen would have never wept
And this paper would have never absorbed
The intensity of what my heart feels

Somewhere on the edge of paradise
Where an aquamarine sea of tranquility
Cuddles powder pink sand,
Lovers rendezvous
Coconut trees provide a cozy shade
While a live band serenades
An intimate dance of merengue takes place

In the distance seagulls play their dance of prey
While our bodies tangle
Like strangers acting like lovers
Engaged in a sultry tango
This atmosphere I'll create for you

Because you make it feel like December 25th
I've never experienced anything like this
Inside of me is a child
Excited to unwrap my gift
With every beat you flow through my heart
And I thank God for bringing you to me
I rest assured until our lips kiss
With no pretense
I welcome this...serendipity

awakening the other side

awakening the other side

Let Me Love You

Day after day it gets harder
Because I need you near
I want to feel every aspect of your being
Let me show you how much I care
Words can't explain
But it can be felt through my touch

What must I do to get next to you?
I'm trying to pull you close
But the resistance is stronger than my persistence
I question why
Do you want to feel the pleasures of a natural high?
Wonderful this can only be
Time has proved sincerity
Can you see this is destiny?

My eyes want visions of only you
Like an eclipse, I want you to block my view
Let me taste the tears you cry
To kiss your eyelids dry
Let my lips touch the tip of your earlobe
To whisper all the things of you I adore
No need to fret, I'll make you feel secure
Better yet, I can show you better than I can tell you
That's for sure

Love Js Blind

Love, I'm missing you
Is it absence that makes the heart grow fonder?
Because love, I can't take this any longer
I say, the presence of love
Makes the heart grow stronger
To feel love with all your senses enhances
Loves' many channels one to infinity,
Which depends on the degree of intimacy

I want to touch you, as if I was blind
From your face to your toes
To picture you inside out, with my eyes closed
Like a feather gently tracing your body,
Every line, every curve
Sensations will rush to your spine,
To awaken every nerve

Kisses to follow to savor every bit of you
Stare into your eyes to your soul,
Because that's where you are whole
Whisper to your spirit, where you are true,
The essence of love is upon you

Not infatuation because love has no obsessions
Love is pure without flaws and it's about trust
Not to be confused or mistaken with lust
Lust is pain locked with chains,
And leads to corruption, but love is correction
Serve with protection
And carries the key to set you free

I look through spiritual eyes
Pass disguises and all décor
To see the bare, straight to the soul
Which is you stripped to the core
Only reading what the heart says
Because it's love with you I want to share

Do not be led by stipulation
Look deeper into your situation,
You'll see lust is the cause of all complications,
Jealousy, envy and hate
So renew the mind to liberate

awakening the other side

Catch Afire

Born at different times, years apart
Yet we were sent to be joined
To accomplish what was signed
The fire that is burning
Cannot be quenched
The mission of love will recompense
I can't walk away
Because the fire that keeps me alive
It's the same fire that drives
And this fire is burning

Trying to bring back the love
Society is losing
Little by little, one by one,
We can start by getting rid of all the guns,
On our streets away from our kids
Show them another way that they can beat,
Their anger and frustration
Find a solution to their complications

But first let's start with the mind
To change the outlook
So there will be no more kinds of,
Fingers pulling triggers and all the lives it took
Let the force of unity be throughout our community
Let's rise above the mediocrity,
Because we're all conquerors through love

And this fire is burning but it doesn't consume me
But some get burned, caught up in the heat of passion
They don't think for a second that they could lose their
     lives,
Without using protection

awakening the other side

And this fire is burning
For our neighbors' streets that are crying
And for the thousands that are dying
Meanwhile some turn their heads away
Thinking it's too big to overcome
But it starts with you
From one comes many, to get the job done

And this fire is burning
For this is not a competition
We're all in this together
Whatever the path,
All have been given seeds for sowing
But some try to get all they can
They don't care about the other man
They are blind to the fact that helping others
Is the nourishing aid to our crops growing
We'll eat the fruits of our seeds,
By every measure of our deeds

Instead of pulling down, let's lift up one another
So we can all get to where we're going
Because when we die, we'll leave all behind
All headed for the same direction,
One day to face judgment

And this fire is burning
For the ones who hurt
There is hope and the sun is shining
Somewhere underneath all the dirt,
All the mire that you sink in
And there is a Man who'll lend you a hand
To pull you to a level ground where you are able to stand
This fire is burning and will continue to burn
Until Love rectifies this land

Mask

Sleepless nights moving in the direction of every light
Pushing, pulling, everyone is taking a bite of the sweet
    delight
Monochrome even when colorful,
Empty even when plentiful

Don't be drunk of this world
And neglect the times
But you can be sober even when sipping on wine
Watch and pray that you don't stray
Into a wilderness
Turning your light into darkness

Set your course, steady the pace of your feet,
Don't move at this world's rapid heart beat
No need to rush or shove
Learn how to decipher through disguises
Because many are wearing masks
They're not even aware of

awakening the other side

A Cry In The Dark

On a horse traveling high on a mountain
I heard a cry in the dark
I can see lights of a small town from afar
As I approach, my heart starts pounding
Because now the cry is resounding

Into a window I peep
Before my eyes I see
A lady on her knees
Bent over as she weeps
Startled by the sounds of my horse
She looked up to see who was there
Behold the beauty my eyes steal
My eyes pierced her soul
I hid myself for reasons I can't explain
I've fallen for her as I felt her pain

Who is there? Her soft tender voice I hear
My presence, I now must make her know
So I stood up to let myself show
I replied, I've heard your cry
And I've followed it for miles
What is it that has caused you harm
And has taken away your smile?
May I be of assistance to aid your dismal?

She replied, I'm accused of a crime I didn't commit
By trial tomorrow I'll be sentenced to death
I have nowhere to run or hide
I answered with urgency, for this lady I can't let die

Don't stress, you I'll rescue
Take only your necessity
On my horse I'll take you with me
A distant land I journey to
There you'll be safe and have all you need
In a green meadow that sits by the sea

awakening the other side

Destiny

This is bigger than you and me
Nothing can come in between
For the door is open
And I'm walking through,
To what has already been approved

Make every moment count
Yesterday is gone,
And tomorrow who knows what will come
Through the spirit I see with signs I'm guided
For what is to be, can't be undone

So all we have is here and now
I put my trust in The Almighty Hands
To walk this land in the direction
Fulfilling my purpose, with possible distractions
But whatever the situation there is a solution

Life experience is preparation
Even disappointments are on my side,
Teaching and moving me to new insights
I will not worry I release to be free
Because some things are meant to be

Nothing stops or blocks
The pathway to my destined place
The dream will not sleep
My destiny awaits
Because I can see it looking back at me
I do more than speak, I prophesy
For what is mine God will provide

awakening the other side

I will not fear what lies ahead
When darkness comes
The light will shine bright,
Illuminating the way for me
So I can continue my journey
To my destiny

awakening the other side

Haunting Confusion

Entering my mind like a broken dam
Flooding my internal being
Washing away my sanity
Making me a prisoner to my thoughts
Lost in the forest of my mind

With emotions wrestling belief
Of what I want to be true
But it is what it is, what it will be
Dense like a bottomless sea
Fragile like slipping memory

In dreams containing you eternally
I leave my reality there
Hearts bleeding pain are dyed with euphoria
I ride nostalgia like a horse running free
Till the bitter is tasty
With melancholy whistling sweet melodies
Like air through my hair

When I awaken to the soft face of morning
A prayer to help ascertain
Plunge into nothing to something
To a world where I'm always sane
I'm wishing to embrace the arms of slumber again and
    again

awakening the other side

Journey

So many times I've searched to find love
In and out of relationships
Bruised and burned
All the struggles and heartaches
Leave me bitter and drained
All the roads I've taken
Led me to nowhere
Dead end places, two sided faces
I throw my hands in the air
Scream, I can't take this!

Chasing dreams that seem unreachable
Momentary schemes are not what it takes,
To have what is attainable for me
Broken down from every blow,
The doors shut tight in my face
But I keep knocking though
Persisting to find my way to a better place
Somewhere down the road, I've made a wrong turn
Faced with this concern should I continue straight ahead
      or return

Walking a straight line gets harder every day
Clever disguises try to block my pathway
Pulling me towards I need not go
I close my eyes, pray, Lord please guide my way
Strengthen me so I won't collide
Secure my path, so I don't fall by the wayside
I won't faint, I'll stand strong
Because He takes that walk with me all along

Stand Still

I stand still as the worlds swirl
Time elapsed and I walked in slow motion
Like my spirit walked on particles passed through atoms
Penetrated into another dimension
Watching this world carry on as usual
Artificial highs, zombies flooded my eyes
Mother Nature cried in a whisper
But busy ears do not hear
Like a fly buzzing on a hot summer's day
Being a nuisance pulling away like a distraction
Even though my eyelids fell to rest
I still did see
Whose eyes did I look through?
Maybe I stood there looking from eternity

awakening the other side

Unselfish Love

Fear stops our faith
If we're afraid to move out
Of our comfortable state of mind
We allow this deceiving world to dictate
How we think, talk and feel
If only we can get our minds out of this world,
See beyond

Until we learn to love as if we were blind
From our hearts and not from our eyes
Our perception won't enslave us
We won't be blind to the deception and lies,
There'll be no separation or nullification
Only unification because we won't be in that state of
    mind
But this is the plan of the mastermind who deceives
To strip us of what we are really meant to be

Seems like the only reason to love
Is to gratify ourselves
What can you do for me?
How you should make me feel
There is no sacrifice
Love me this way or leave

But there are some who bring
The Kingdom of God from above
Down to Earth to implement the new birth
The day will come when we stand in unity as one
All one under a loving Father
You're my sister and you're my brother
If the truth surpasses your understanding
Stop trying to make sense of things
And just believe in Love

Deliverance

Things must come
Wars and much more
Prophecies will be
Every believer already sees
Through revelation
So pray for mercy in this day
For all that was mentioned
Your redeemer will obey
So do not fear
Your life has been determined without blame
For eternal life was given
Manifested when Jesus came
And the promise is yours to claim

Look to the future, move with inspiration
Which comes from our Heavenly Father
Set yourself free and stop living in slavery
Trust in God, stop worrying about them
Because no one escapes the judgment of Him
For they are not in control and they know not what
    they do
But God is working for the good of you

God is everywhere so become one with all
His love, let nature recall
Listen to the whisper a message in the arms of the wind
His breath brushing like rose petals against your skin
Whistling like when the morning birds sing
Telling you of the deepest sense of devotion
An array of peace will sit in your emotion
That lets your mind drift like a leaf on the ocean

awakening the other side

Your spirit will fly like with eagle wings
High in the sky to embrace heaven
Where time stops in motion
To meet the Creator of Creation
To you, salvation is given
And angels welcoming you to the celebration

awakening the other side

There Is None Greater

There is none greater
None better than the grace
You've given me
For your love is forever
It's with you I wanna stay
The rest of my days

You are the love of my life
The breath I breathe you've given to me
You've unlocked my destiny
For only you carry the key
You are everything
You're now until eternity

You've been there all the while,
Showing me the way
Holding my hands through my troubled times
Even though I didn't obey
Didn't pray like I ought to
Call on you like I should
But you love me anyway

When my world is upside down,
You turn it around
You're my backbone, you heal my wounds
There's no place I'd rather be
Than walking side by side,
Abiding in you, and you in me

I pray I remain humble unto you
For nothing in this world can separate your love from me
No mountain or sea can come in between
I'll love you until my dying day
When that time comes, I'll see your smiling face

awakening the other side

awakening the other side

Destiny Course

It doesn't matter where you stand
No one can take away what is yours
For your destiny is uniquely defined
And the key is in God's hands
To unlock all the doors
Your light is yours to shine
So let it radiate with joy
For where you're going
It's a choice you'll have to make
To determine the path you'll take

For nothing can get in your way
Even when obstacles stand tall
Speak the spoken words and they shall fall
Out of many are called only God knows the sum
The challenges may be hard
But with Love in your heart you'll overcome

Every thing you say and do
A portrait of your life is produced
A sculpture of you is what you mold
Painted by your life's episode
The negative eats it away like a disease
The positive is the remedy
Which carves it into the masterpiece

Imitate the image of God in all your ways
Inside we all carry a divine trait
A new you, you'll create
The roads you'll travel will be bright like day
For His words are faithful and true
The desires of your heart were promised you
You can reap the rewards if you obey

Let hate be absent for your sisters and brothers
We're all born from the same Father
So let us Love one another

awakening the other side

Infectious

If seeing is believing then your impossible
Will never be, if what you perceive is what you believe
Then that's what you will receive
If blind how do you dream?
How can you recognize what you've never seen?
So seek God who makes the impossible real
You'll get a glimpse of what is unseen
Awakening what is so inwardly keen

Too many shallow minds like an empty well
Are leading the blind
These voices are infecting this generation
Through devil devices are the invasion
All these intoxications are causing mental disturbance
No moral values are being put on self
Like moral values are being pushed to the back of a shelf

While all this stares you in the face
Even this has its place
Can prayers change prophecy?
These things envisioned before the century
We must light the pathway so all can see
We carry the torch because victory is ours
Even our whispers speak loud with power
We can use the same devices but to heal the scars

Face In The Crowd

Not typical but mystical
Not acting like the usual
Simple yet complex
The things of this world in my heart I don't want to find
Because heaven bound is of my mind
A steady stare through my eyes a mirror reflects
Ancient tales of what once lived

Images of the future revealed in the present
Before they happen like déjà vu
Theses broken scenes I saw I knew

The end was known before the beginning
Perhaps this tale I glimpse
But only on a lower scale
It's too much for my carnal mind to comprehend
And not paying attention makes me miss
What He reveals before it happens

He walks with the lowly
Yet puts to shame the high and mighty
A Prince but in disguise
His face will you recognize
If he comes next to you and sits
How will you treat him?
His camouflage can be any face you come in contact
    with

What will you do if the world changes tomorrow?
Buying and selling no longer the way you know it
A number given to all members for their dealings
All to protect their earnings, they are systematically
 coded
This is a false security but the blind won't know it
Controlling though all means of manipulation
However money won't make a difference in the time of
Tribulation

Expressions of Love

My heart is bursting with love
Like clouds burdened with tears
I'm walking through a meadow
Full of lilies and daffodils
I'm seeing blue skies revealing this paradise
Even the weeping willow won't cry

A river carries my pain as she goes
Happy creeps up then carries me
Into the ocean arms of ecstasy
Peacefully I rest like on a bed of roses
Reflections of heaven in my eyes, shows

Joy lifts me to a mountain peak
High above the valley, where worry strolls
Waiting for me to carry his load
But I wait on the wind to catch my wing
So I can soar, where worry can't pressure me any more

While the sun conceals his kiss
My blues skies disappear
Leaving shades of red and lavender exposed
I cling to the moon to be composed awaiting my dreams
Because there you will appear as real as it seems

Tomorrow

The rhythm of the moon drives the tide
Upon his back I take a ride
While beating the wind not to be tossed from side to
    side
Kismet welcomes me with a wave of its hand
Like a lighthouse eyes being shone
To the shore where I belong

In search of aspiration
Disembarking on a strange land
Everyday looking for tomorrow
For my future, which already is
Making it sometimes seem like a delay
Even though inevitably tomorrow may come
My future is today and today

What do I do now?
My certainty is in the present parallel to my dreams
Breathing through hope
With every second is a miracle
Outweighing any obstacle
Cascading the glory of the sun
The promise of the new day to come
Maybe here or there
Somewhere, my guarantee already

awakening the other side

Epilogue

Naked Truth

Wonderfully garnished she stands enduring the wear and tear of blistering heat. The coolness of rain revives allowing her to stretch her limbs relishing her beauty. Then fall leaves her stripped and the coldness is brutal on her bones. After the harsh reality of what she undergoes that season passes and the splendor begins again. Wonderfully garnished she stands enduring the wear and tear of the blistering heat, but the essence of her true beauty is not seen in her flourishing leaves; it is while she stands naked what transpires underneath.

About the Author

Michelle Hanna, a
native of the
Bahamas moved to
Florida in 1991.
Since that time she
has accumulated
the accolades of
her spiritual self. A
quest but not a
new one rather one of her lifetime. However for the past
two years her life has undergone a more spiritual awakening experience through the many incidences that have
transpired, which led her to this destination of the outpouring of her heart into poetry. As a youngster she has
always been fascinated with the matters of the heart and
mind, which has sparked her interest in Psychology and
Metaphysics to better understand these aspects of life. Her
realizations have extended to real life experiences of love,
sorrow, pain, longings, hopes and dreams, not only from
her life but also from what she has seen around her by putting herself into another person's shoes to get a better
understanding from their point of view. Through her jour-

ney of self-value and true inspiration she encourages you to awaken the other side within. With *Awakening The Other Side* she is hoping to achieve just that, to awaken the other side of thinking, understanding, love, empathy and your spiritual self. Come, let us experience and understand life through your eyes from her eyes.

Acknowledgments

Thanks and praise to the Creator of all things, The Almighty God, for the purpose and plans which were sent before me. The inspiration that flowed from my heart onto these pages is the result of the grand schemes of situations that occurred in my life. The synchronicity of the past two years has been amazing, from one thing to another. There's a reason for everything that happens, and I'm thankful for the positioning of every person at the right moment that help sparked this fire, thank you. Many blessings to my family, God couldn't have chosen a better family for me. To my parents, thank you for what you've instilled in me; I'm forever thankful and I cherish you all. To my adopted family, true friendship is a rarity and I'm blessed to have sincere people in my life. We are forever bonded and words can't express my appreciation and gratitude.

Special thanks to:

Nikki Giovanni, many thanks to you for a beautifully written foreword. My heart is singing. I pray to God that He continues to use your voice.

73

Eriq LaSalle, thank you for your expressive honesty.

NPIPB, all of you are forever in my heart.

Don Parchment, your inner eyes reflect through your photographs, thank you.

Ayesha Bernardo, thank you for doing what you do to make things happen.

La Toya Atkins, thank you for your creative eyes.

To every person who has read, listened and commented with honesty, many thanks and appreciation to you. To everyone else who has played their part in the creation of this book, many thanks to you.

All of you are a part of this dream, now reality.

God bless you all,
Michelle

First Line Index

Artist Index